*****

Father Beiting's previous CAP books include:

God Can Move Mountains

Appalachia...a Special Place . . . A Bridge of Hope

Promises To Keep . . . A Vision for Appalachia

Dreams of Faith

*Called to the Mountains . . . The Autobiography of
Father Ralph W. Beiting*

Frontier of the Heart . . . The Search for Heroes in America

*Pilgrimage of a Country Preacher . . . A Journey to the Holy
Land of Appalachia*

Copies of these books can be obtained by writing to:

Christian Appalachian Project
322 Crab Orchard Road
Lancaster, KY 40446-0001

TABLE OF CONTENTS

Page

DEDICATION

To whom should one dedicate a book about family? My parents quickly come to mind. Grandparents, aunts, uncles, brothers and sisters, cousins, nieces and nephews all call out to be remembered, and justly so.

But as I try to put words in order and express my gratitude, another thought comes to me—one that transcends blood lines and race.

My thoughts go back to the beginning of the Christian family, to the Holy Family, my ideal of family life: Mary, the beautiful maid of Nazareth . . . Joseph, the young carpenter of Galilee . . . Jesus, son of Mary and God.

These three were the foundation and the light of all future families. To them—to Mary, Joseph, and Jesus—I dedicate this small book.

Their life of love, sacrifice, and dedication has inspired me from my youth. Because of this Holy Family, we have the hope and the conviction that we can all be the Family of God. To the Holy Family I give my life, my strength, and my thanks.

The Christian Appalachian Project
1964-1996

More than forty years ago, Father Ralph W. Beiting was called to Appalachia to build church communities and ease the pain caused by poverty. In 1964, he founded an interdenominational Christian organization called the Christian Appalachian Project (CAP). By offering long-term, self-help solutions to the problems that hold Appalachia's people back, CAP gives the poor a chance to work themselves out of poverty and to see themselves as they truly are: the people of God.

CAP provides educational programs for children and adults, home repair assistance, business-development programs, elderly visitation programs, emergency relief assistance, and so many other efforts. With over seventy programs and activities, CAP brings hope and peace to those in need.

Through the generous work of thousands of volunteers, hundreds of local workers, and a host of loyal supporters from all over the country, CAP has become one of the largest relief organizations in America, and a pioneer in the development of programs to defeat poverty and inspire hope.

Prologue—Building the Family of God

A number of years ago I was street preaching in a very rural part of Leslie County, Kentucky. When I finished speaking, I went to get a soft drink at the little general store. I came out of the store and sat on the porch where a young boy was sitting in a rocking chair. We chatted for a few moments and I asked him, "What do you want to be when you grow up?"

Without a moment's hesitation he answered, "I want to be like my pap."

I thought to myself, what a wonderful ambition! What a wonderful goal! It took me back to when I was just a little older than that boy and I wanted to be like my "pap."

He was the father of eleven children. He was a carpenter, and loved to build beautiful and useful things. He planted gardens and saw things grow. He raised chickens. He played baseball and was a pretty good pitcher.

He kissed my mother when he left home in the morning and when he came home in the evening. He played with us kids and taught us so much. He went to church and he truly loved to pray.

Yes, I very much wanted to be like my pap.

In high school, I began to wonder about my vocation—what I would do with my life. I thought I'd like to be an architect and to have a dozen kids like my dad. Building homes and building a family seemed a noble dream—so clean, so sharp, so fine.

Then a priest did me in.

This priest was one of my teachers in high school. One day, when I was a junior, he asked me to stay after school for a short talk. I assumed it was going to be about an English assignment that I hadn't done well enough.

He didn't want to talk about English at all. "What do you want to be?" he asked me. I told him of my idea to be an architect and raise a family. He said, "I think you aren't listening to your heart. I think you should be a priest."

Now I liked priests. I thought them special, but perhaps a little extreme. They had no family of their own, no children. Who would want to pay such a price to be a priest? But because I appreciated this priest—and maybe to get out of an awkward spot—I told him I would think about it.

"Do more than that," he said. "I want you to pray about it." I agreed to do that. That's what started all the trouble.

I prayed, and I prayed, and prayed again, hoping each time for a different answer, but by the time senior classes began, I felt sure that God was asking me to be a priest. "But I want to have a family. And what about when you said to our first parents in the Bible, 'Be fruitful and multiply'?" I asked God. I got no answer from God but the simple direction to keep going, to go on.

God is often like that. He can be irritating. He gives directions but doesn't always answer our questions, at least not right away.

As I reflect now, I'm sure that God must have smiled that day when I asked Him about being fruitful and multiplying and having a dozen kids. He must have smiled because He had more than one family in mind for me—and He who knew the future knew I'd have more than a dozen kids.

Tens of thousands would call me Father!

You have to be careful with God. When you ask for something, you had better be prepared to get even more than you ask for.

I am now 72 years old. Forty-seven years of priesthood have been written down and recorded. Forty-six years as a missionary in the Appalachian mountains have come and gone and yet the journey has not yet ended. At times like today, I think it has hardly begun. So much remains to be accomplished. But the memories of my family keep me strong.

I remember the day my parents, old and dying, saw each other for the last time. My father was in a nursing home and my mother was dying of cancer. She wanted to see my father one more time, and thank goodness, we were able to bring her to the nursing home to be near him. My mother was settled in a special room and we wheeled my father in his chair to her bedside. Little did we know that in less than ten minutes, my mother would be home with God.

When my father looked at her, my mother reached out and held his hand and looked into his eyes.

"Daddy," she said, "you know I have always loved you and I love you so today."

I said the prayers for the dying, and said "Amen." Then she closed her eyes.

My brothers and sisters and their wives and husbands held hands. They cried unashamedly, offering each other their strength even as they leaned on each other in sorrow. For such is family.

My grandfather and grandmother died within a month of one another. They were simple people, hard working, and surely temples of God from which grace came in great abundance. They enriched our lives so very much.

Now, all my parents' brothers and sisters are gone, except one. My Uncle Bill is partially paralyzed and hasn't been able to work for nearly twenty-five years. But he is still full of joy because his wife Mary loves him and cares for him.

My brother Ray, next behind me, is gone. My cousin Gene has passed away, and even my nephew Kevin has died. Several newly born nieces and nephews were taken to the Lord when they had hardly begun to live.

My family, both alive and dead, formed and fashioned me. The nobler gifts are theirs. Because of their example I have come to see how truly important and beautiful family life can be.

In the fall of 1950 when I put down roots for a lifetime of service to Appalachia, I found strong families. For example, I found a family whose mother was dying of cancer. She had five little children— the oldest wasn't even ten. Her husband, Nicholas, was a simple man who worked in the coal mines. When I heard about them, I stopped by, a stranger, to see if I could help.

Nicholas said, "Would you pray?" As I did, I thought to myself, how in the name of God can he hold on so strong and see his wife gradually but surely sink into death? When she died six weeks later, he was left with all those kids. Yet he saw to it that all those children were cared for and that they were with family, and he was their support and their life.

There was abundant love and life in that family— and there still is. To this day, I receive letters from Nicholas.

I think, too, of the man I met on the road one Christmas Day, walking in nearly eight inches of snow to a town five miles away. He told me he was going to cut firewood from a tree that had fallen in the storm, determined to have a fire for his children and his wife on Christmas. He later told me that the seven of them gathered around that warm fire and had a wonderful time of family love on Christmas.

These were both strong families. Families whose parents refused to walk away and quit.

I remember Jessie and Maggie, two elderly people. I visited their home every Monday evening and sat around the potbelly stove to tell stories of God and the scriptures. I asked them what they had done in their lives that had made them happy. Their response was simple: They had raised a large family and they were grandparents. They had given the world a family of values and strength. What more could one ask?

Then there was a woman who came to my house to ask for food. She had walked seven miles because she had absolutely nothing to feed her children—

not even a potato or a slice of bread. I was amazed at her dedication. She never thought of leaving her children and going her own way and neither did her husband. They would stick through it all.

All of these folks and many more like them left behind a strong and secure people. Divorce was not an acceptable way out for any of them. They cared and they loved in good times and in bad. The children knew only one set of parents and therefore had the strength to build something strong and permanent with their lives.

Forty-six years after I first came to Appalachia, the picture has changed. In so short a time family life is in tatters. Divorce is a reality for nearly one out of two couples. Spouse and child abuse are almost epidemic in our mountains. The number of children who will never know their own fathers is increasing. Grandparents are left to fend for themselves in loneliness and despair.

Where God and the Bible and church were once the hallmarks of a mountain family, today only a small percentage of the people go to church. The Bible can no longer compete with television or sports or fashion magazines.

Today, family life needs resurrection.

I think God is saying to me, "Now more than ever before, be a father, help me rebuild the families of

Appalachia." Somehow I must succeed. Surely, I have to try. To do that, I must look to my family.

Twenty-five years ago I was selected by a national group as the outstanding volunteer in America. Whether that was accurate, only God knows. But it did make me realize how truly important volunteers are. They have become so essential a part of my real family. Thousands of them have joined me in the last forty-six years.

They have assisted me in ways I could never have asked them to do. They have given when I was convinced there was no more to give. Even when they return to their own families, they keep me and the people of the mountains in their hearts—in their families. When I travel I stay at their houses. I eat at their tables. I pray with them in the sanctuary of their homes. They are a strength and a bond that only family can give.

Beyond sight, across the valleys and plains of this great country, are thousands more who support the work I do. They write such beautiful letters to me. They send me cards on feast days and holidays. They pray. They make sacrifices so that I can better care for the family of God.

Recently I was in Boston giving a presentation to a group of former CAP volunteers and their friends and families. One handed me a card from an eighty-five-year-old woman. She had been a supporter of mine for thirty-five years but was unable to come to the meeting. The volunteers asked me to call her and talk with her.

I did, and I was impressed by that wonderful lady. She told me that for thirty-five years, she had gathered clothing for the poor, sorted it, packed it, and sent it to Appalachia. She had also sent donations whenever she could.

She told me how disappointed she was that she was unable to attend the presentation. As I hung up the phone I said to myself, "Surely, I have a mother still."

Now I'm dedicating the last years of my life to strengthening and rebuilding the families, not only of Appalachia, but of all those whose shadow has fallen upon me and my life.

In the chapters that follow I hope to tell the story of family—and how together, through it and its Christian dimensions, we can still build the City of God.

A Young Man's Start in Appalachia

When you are young, an excitement always seems to fill your soul. As you grow independent of your parents, you become breathtakingly aware of being an individual.

Perhaps because of that, you tend to focus on individual issues and challenges.

At least, that was the way it was for me, as a young priest beginning a journey in Appalachia.

I'd see a problem or a challenge and would rush in to solve it. I'd try to fix what first presented itself—what first came to my mind.

In many things, however, the family is wiser than the individual. The elders are wiser than the child. It would be some time before I learned this lesson—and learned to see as the father of all families sees.

What I saw, in those early years, brought great sorrow to my heart.

Quite often, as I drove the twisting mountain roads,

I'd see a creek defiled by trash—from old wrecked abandoned cars to discarded refrigerators. Their hulks crowded those creeks and streams. When children played there, they risked cutting themselves on the rusted cars or making an icebox their airless tomb.

My heart ached for those children. I wondered what I could do to give them a decent place to play, a place to be safe - a place just to be ordinary kids.

One day I confronted a young boy who had stolen a bicycle. He said, "Yes. I stole the bike."

"Why?" I asked.

"Because I wanted to be like everybody else."

"You mean because everybody else steals?"

"No, because everyone else has something. I don't have nothing. I saw that bike and I thought I ought to be able to have one. I took it because I wanted to be like everybody else. I didn't want to be the oddball."

Another time, I took a group of boys on an outing. One boy told me he hated his mother. I said, "How can you say you hate your mother? Mothers are people of love."

"Mine ain't," he said. "When I was little she put my head in the toilet bowl and flushed the toilet to make me drown. I reckon I would have, too, if my grandma hadn't come by and pushed my Ma aside and pulled me out. Now my Daddy has run off and

Ma has another man, and the man don't like me."

There was a young girl with deep, deep problems. She was the oldest of five children. Her mother was very ill. Her father was trying desperately to make enough money in the coal fields to keep them all alive.

This twelve-year-old girl had to bathe her mother and dress her every day, fix the meals for the family, and do all the other household chores.

Exhaustion and stress were denying this child her childhood—and finally she came to the end of her strength. One day, in desperation, she took a pillow and put it over her mother's face, thinking this would end the family's problems. Fortunately, the father came upon the scene and pulled the pillow away before the mother died, but the poor, shattered girl would never be the same.

Out of all these tragedies with children came my plans to start a summer camp. I wanted to take care of these children. I wanted to give them a place to play where they would be able to be kids and not be overburdened with so many adult tragedies.

If I could start a camp, and bring the children in and talk to them around the campfire at night, and let them know that people cared and loved and were willing to help, then maybe . . . maybe they would remember. Maybe they would persevere. Maybe they would find a better tomorrow.

Well, with the help and prayers of my family of friends and volunteers, I have just begun Camp Daniel Boone, the fifth camp that I've started in these mountains. Now each summer, hundreds more kids will have the opportunity to see another kind of life, to make new friends, to meet caring counselors from all over the country—and to know joy and laughter and hope.

Over the years, there were so many times that I answered the door to find a parent asking for food and clothing. The children had nothing to eat. Winter was only a snowstorm away. They didn't have warm winter clothing. Even more important, the clothes they had were so out of style and so tattered that the children didn't want to go to school because the other kids would tease them.

There was so much that these families lacked. They often had no bedding or towels. Simple necessities like dishes or pots and pans, were scarce.

I knew that our summer camps only gave the children a respite from their harsh lives. I had to do something to help their families.

I decided to start second-hand stores, to give families a place to buy the necessities of life at prices they could afford—without sacrificing their pride.

The "store" started out in the front yard of my

church as a rope tied between two trees, on which we hung clothing. Sometimes it was a box or crate put out in the shade of the tree, filled with household items.

Before long, it was obvious that our "store" would need protection from the weather. With the help and prayers of my great and wonderful family of friends and volunteers, I made permanent homes for what we came to call our "Attic Stores." Sometimes we rented buildings, other times we bought them or built them from the ground up.

Often, once an Attic Store is established, we turn it over to the local community. Last year, more than 46,000 men, women, and children came away from our Attics with clothing and the other necessities for simple human dignity.

It wasn't only the children and young families who needed help, however.

Early in my ministry I made it my goal to visit every household in the counties assigned to me. As I went from door to door I found so many elderly men and women living alone, huddled in small, dark, and cold corners of run-down shacks.

When I saw their loneliness and fear and remembered my own parents and grandparents, I knew I had to do something.

Out of these powerful experiences I began our Elderly Services program. We set up regular visits to the homes of our seniors. We took them to the doctor and to the grocery store. We sat with them and read them letters, and the Bible, and did whatever we could to lighten their hearts.

We still do this. Last year, we served 731 elders in 11 counties. In helping them and comforting them in these small ways, we restore a little of the sense of family that is missing from their lives.

Many times over the years, people have come to me to ask for wood or coal or to have the gas turned on when the mercury is near zero. All they're asking is to stay warm for at least a little while. How could I refuse them? How could I say, "I don't want to leave the warmth of my house to come out into the cold where you are?"

What can I say to a mother who has walked miles to get food for her crying children? Do I tell her, "Sorry, but I'm tired, and the day is nearly over, and there have been so many here before you"?

When I'm tempted to turn them away, I remember what Jesus said: "I was hungry and you gave me food, I was thirsty and you gave me drink."

I also realized, however, that I couldn't care for everyone myself.

That's why we created Outreach Services. We help people buy food, pay the electric bill, or buy medicine. Usually, we ask people to repay the favor by volunteering in one of our programs, and often they have. We brighten their lives and give them a little bit of hope, and they spread that hope to others.

My father was a carpenter and so were his father and grandfather before him. Much of my young life was spent working at their sides, helping to build a chicken house or a stable, or repairing the school or the church buildings.

When I came to Appalachia, I saw some of the poorest housing in the nation. I saw people living in old abandoned garages, and school buses, and dilapidated trailers.

The leaky roofs, the lack of running water or electricity, the outhouses brought a sorrow to my heart that had to be answered. The carpenter in me cried out, "What are we going to do?"

Our Home Repair program grew from that carpenter's voice in my head. Using donated materials and volunteer labor, we made run-down houses safe and warm again.

At first the satisfaction of doing these things filled me with joy. I pointed with pride to how many people we had helped in all these new programs.

But it wasn't long before I began to be troubled by doubt. No matter how many folks we helped, dozens more suffered the same need. I kept saying to myself, "Will the problems never end? Will the lines never go away? Will the knocks on my door never cease?"

Even more troubling than the enormity of the problem was that the same people I helped one day were back at my door the next. They'd eaten the food. They'd worn out the clothes. Their house was cold again. Their loneliness was still there.

I thought to myself, "Have I gone down the wrong path? Have I climbed the wrong mountain? What am I doing wrong?"

In spite of my desperation, I had the good sense to pause. As I thought this through, I realized that I had to go to someone greater, wiser, more resourceful than I.

The youth who had rushed out to solve every problem needed the advice of his Father.

I spent a great deal of time in prayer. I prayed as I drove countless miles in the course of my ministry. I prayed in the quiet of my church. I prayed at home during those brief moments of relaxation at the end of the day. I kept calling out, "Speak to me, Lord. Tell me what to do. Show me the way."

Slowly but surely He opened my eyes and my heart. He reminded me that the older brothers and sisters of a family don't just carry the little ones—they help them learn to walk.

He reminded me that the members of a family don't just lean on each other—they prop each other up. They offer strength. They give as well as receive.

They grow together.

The Lord allowed me to see the people here not as individuals needing help from crisis to crisis, but as members of a family ready and willing to help each other, and needing only the tools.

We are all family. That family is the channel of God's love, God's goodness, and His healing power—for the individual, and for the world.

God, give me the vision to see as You see, and the strength to do as You do. Help me to have the wisdom to teach families to help themselves.

The Vision I Was Given

No matter who we are or what we do—whether it's as individuals, as communities, or as governments—we are family. God has shown me that only when we recognize this and act accordingly, will we succeed as we all desire.

Early in my ministry, I used to rise early each day and hurry off to answer the call of the poor. Then I realized something more was needed. I began to devote the first hour of each morning to prayer.

I heard God say, "Take up and read." I knew He meant the Scriptures. I started at the beginning, with the Book of Genesis.

There I rediscovered His bounty. There was the sea and all the creatures it contained. There was the land and the untold treasures buried within it. Animals roamed the earth, birds filled the air, and flowers and trees reached toward the sun and the stars. The harmony and order of the universe was a marvel. In the midst of this beauty stood the most wonderful creature of them all, one who could both know and love: a human being.

Adam was the crown in this universe of splendor. Yet somehow all the beautiful and wonderful things around him weren't enough. He was sad and lonely.

So the Lord cast a sleep upon him. When the man awoke, he found someone even more beautiful than himself. He called her Woman. They fell in love and the human family was born.

God created family not merely for the good of Adam and Eve, or for the children to come. He gave family the task of looking after the earth and keeping it a place of beauty and love. The gift of family was the channel through which God could touch the earth and keep it whole.

The joy did not last, however. Sin prevailed, and beauty and love disappeared.

So God decided to remake the earth. When He was done, he restored beauty and love through a family: that of Noah, his wife, and their three sons and their wives.

How wonderful, I thought, that God re-entered the world through family.

As I read on, the story took on the darker side once more, with hate, greed, violence, and selfishness rising anew. Yet God was determined that human beings should have peace and joy. In the fullness of time He sent His Son, born of a woman, to form the most perfect family the world has ever seen.

The Holy Spirit and Mary, a young Jewish maiden, brought about a new and eternal life. Joseph, a good and just man, became husband and foster father and God gave the Holy Family to the earth. Joseph represented all of us, brought into this wonderful Family of God through dedication and love. The Son redeemed us and allowed us all to join that Family.

As I lay the book down, I realized where I had fallen short.

I had tried to end poverty and bring peace with material things—and it could not be done. I knew I couldn't neglect the hurt and the want that came to each of the individual members of the human family. I had to go beyond the individual. I had to remember the vision—the gift of family.

I remember two young boys I cared about a great deal. They had so little—no yard to play in, no toys of their own. Their clothes were always dirty. I invited them to play in my yard with the neighborhood kids and got each of them a bicycle and some new clothes.

Then I didn't see them for more than a month.

I learned they had been taken away from their parents because of neglect and abuse. When I found out where they were, I went to see the boys in the foster home. I brought them some toys for Christmas and some candy.

It felt good to help those boys, but now they are with their parents again and as poor and lonely as ever. I gave them only things. I didn't fix the family. I didn't help the father and mother. I didn't recognize that only a sound family can end the poverty of these boys.

I think, too, of Jennie, an elderly woman we assist through our Elderly Services program. Elaine, one of our volunteers, became especially close to Jennie. She visited her, took her to doctor's appointments and grocery stores, and helped her with many other needs.

Recently, Elaine completed her year with us and went back to her home in another part of the country. Jennie cried. She said, "Don't you dare let another volunteer come. It breaks my heart when they leave!"

Her words broke my heart. Most of our volunteers are only temporary—we can't change that. We can't promise Jennie that they'll never leave. But Jennie's family lives in a neighboring county. True, they are poor and it is hard for them to visit—but they are the real answer to Jennie's loneliness and need.

Once again, I had forgotten the best solution: family. We are now working hard to get Jennie and her family back together. To the extent we can re-establish the bonds of family, we will end want and bring peace.

I'm not the only one who has made this mistake. At times the welfare system of our country has overlooked family as well. I remember a social worker coming to me one day, asking for help. A family she was working with wouldn't fill out the forms they needed to qualify for assistance.

The social worker said to me, "You've got to convince them to work with me or else they won't get any help at all!"

I went to see the family and said to the mother, "Why can't you make out this list? These are the things they want to know. Why won't you give them to the social worker?"

"Oh," she said, "she treated me like I was a number, a thing. I don't like to be treated like a thing. I like to be treated like I'm folks."

"Like I'm folks"—in other words, "treat me like family."

I do know one example where the different parts of a community came together like family.

Last August, volunteers from Sand Gap Christian Church and CAP worked side by side to repair a home in Jackson County.

Like me, Pastor Gerard Maupin of the Sand Gap

Christian Church is frustrated by the poverty being passed from one generation to the next. He had church elders, deacons, and members eager to pitch in to repair the roof of this home, but he didn't have the necessary materials.

We provided insulation and shingles from our Operation Sharing program. Ross Abrams, who leads CAP's Home Repair crew in Jackson County, volunteered his day off and his expertise to direct Sand Gap's work team. Casey Sterr, a former volunteer and now a CAP employee, also went along.

By the end of the day, the old, uninsulated, leaking tin roof had been completely replaced and the workers knew the deep satisfaction of helping fellow members of God's family.

"In the end," Casey said, "everyone is helped: the people being served, the people doing the work, and the entire local community, drawn together because they show that they care for one another. It is not one group 'doing' for another. Rather it is the support of all involved that leads to growth."

How true that is! Unfortunately, such Christian cooperation on behalf of the family is the exception in this nation, not the rule.

Every religion has admirable qualities. But sometimes we religious leaders try to establish our own turf. We want our own little piece of the action—let the other groups keep their hands off. We are individuals seeking to achieve our own goals.

We fail to remember that the people are not our people, they are God's people. We should be trying to help each other so they can help themselves.

We must learn that while our religious groups are different in many ways, we have to work together as family.

I know that the tensions between some denominations won't be eased overnight. But each day affords us an opportunity to take a step in that direction. Our different beliefs should never prevent us from loving and caring and cooperating with one another. We have to be, surely, the One Family of God.

Individuals also need to be reminded that they are part of that family.

I remember a man named Nathan. Nathan had no religion, and he didn't belong to a church.

One day Nathan's house caught fire. The house was not destroyed, however, and our Outreach Services and other programs helped them reconnect the water and electricity and put their lives back together. We even helped Nathan find a job. He and his wife were extremely grateful.

I didn't see them again for six months. Then I learned that they had moved two counties away. One day later they showed up at my house.

"I'm worse off now than I ever was before," Nathan said. "I have greater loneliness and problems than I ever have known. I don't know what's going to happen."

I said, "You know, we made a mistake. I gave you a job. I gave you a pickup truck. I helped you get your house back. But it wasn't enough. Tell me: Do you love your wife? Does she love you?"

They looked at each other, surprised by my question. "I think we do," he said. "I know we want to."

"Well, that's where we have to begin," I said. "We're going to have to make sure this time that you care for each other and that you are willing to fight for one another, to support one another, to stay with one another."

Then I asked, "What do you think about God?"

Again they looked at each other. He said, "I think we've cheated God. We take what we have and rarely give thanks. We don't go to church. We don't pray. We simply survive. I think we have stolen from God."

"I know you have," I said. "Now, what is your intent today? Will the stealing stop? Will the bonding begin? Will you recognize Him as Father and want to be his Family?"

"Yes," they said. "Yes, we'd like to try."

"You must think about a church," I said then. "I am not asking you to think about mine." (Although I would have been happy if they had!) "You must make up your own mind about where God is calling you. You must respond to His grace."

I asked them to think about this and see me in a week.

At the end of that week, they came and asked, "Can we come in while you pray?" After it was over, we gathered out in the hallway to talk.

Nathan said, "You know, I've been thinking about what you said about God. I have started going to revival meetings. I think I am going to take God as my Savior."

Three days later I saw Nathan again. He told me, "On Sunday afternoon I'm going to be baptized. I've decided to give myself to God. I want to be saved."

His wife said, "I'm going with him, although I am not yet sure that this is the way I should go. But I am going to pray as well."

Then Nathan asked, "Are you disappointed that we didn't join your church?"

"No!" I replied, delighted. "I am so pleased that you have taken God seriously and that you are doing all in your power to get closer to Him. The closer you get to Him, the better family you will have—and the more good will come to you."

That is my dream and my hope—for this family, and for all the families that, in the words of St. Paul, are called to "encourage one another and build one another up." For only then will we build the individual.

When darkness comes at the end of my day—and again, when only an hour is left before the dawn—I try to spend time with my Father. I usually sit on the back porch, something I loved to do when I was a boy.

Lord, thank you for the vision of family that I overlooked for so long. I know now that it is sure and true. I promise I will spend every moment, every effort of my life to make family the center of all that I do and say.

Family: The Wonder Drug for Our Time

It happens too frequently: A young, teen-age mother knocks at my door. She has no husband. Her baby is sick. She doesn't have a car. She lives in a run-down trailer or a small apartment. The rent is due. The utilities are in arrears. She is exhausted and overwhelmed—and in many ways, still only a child herself.

Where do we begin?

The underlying cause of this young mother's desperate situation is not an economic problem. It's a family problem. She is trying to live a life and raise a child in a way not in accordance with God's plan.

God knew, after all, what we human folks need. Beyond all other things, we need both a mother and a father.

One of the most far-reaching causes of poverty and unhappiness in Appalachia is the rising number of unmarried, teen-age mothers.

These young women will constitute the greatest percentage of the poor in the next generation—and two-thirds of their children will live the rest of their lives in poverty.

All this is happening because there is no family.

Recent surveys show that girls brought up without a father in the home are far more sexually active than those whose fathers are present in their lives. This sexual activity leads to even more fatherless children, and the cycle continues.

I was approached not long ago by a married woman with two children, living in a government housing project. She wanted to get an education so she could better support herself and her children, but didn't know how to accomplish that because there was no one to care for the children while she was in school.

I asked about her husband.

"He's in jail," she replied. "He physically abused the children when he got drunk. I had to have him put away for our safety."

In this case, the mother was married, but the father was a threat and an embarrassment to the family. This woman had severe problems.

The solution for both mothers is not just better housing, or even better education. These will contribute to their well-being. But the root problem is a broken family life. Until that is cured, there is no lasting hope. Family is God's given solution.

I know there are social service agencies that have a great desire to help these women. In truth, they often make the problems worse.

Spouse abuse, is an excellent example—a serious and devastating sin. In many cases, social workers recommend separation and immediate divorce.

I want to make it absolutely clear that I do not believe a husband ever, ever has a right to hit his wife. There is no doubt at times that separation is necessary to stop the violence. In fact, we operate two spouse abuse shelters ourselves. We assisted women and children from almost 500 households in crisis last year.

But is shelter alone going to solve the problem? The problem is the family.

The abusing husband has to be a part of the solution. He needs counseling and direction. If at all possible, that couple needs to be brought back together in love and hope.

When our Family Life Services workers take the extra time to provide marriage counseling coupled with prayer and dedication, amazing things often happen.

Yet separation and alienation seem built into our culture today.

Then too, I think parents often believe their major

contribution to their children's future is a material or
an educational gift—instead of the gift of family and
its values.

Fortunately, I have seen exceptions.

A teen-age girl I cared for decided to marry in haste.
For once, it was not a case of pregnancy. I advised
against the marriage because I sensed that they were
just not ready. They were not adequately prepared
for this important step.

They got married anyway. The husband's job took
them nearly a thousand miles from the girl's parents.
In about six months, she wrote to her mother that her
husband was simply awful, and she wanted to come
home.

Her mother wrote back to her daughter. She told
her that her parents' home was no longer her home.
Her home was with her husband. She urged her to
go to the minister of her church and seek counseling.

This story has a happy ending. That once-young
couple has now been married nearly 25 years. They
have raised several wonderful children. The answer
to this young woman's problem was not separation.
It was bonding and unity.

I'm afraid that today, parents might simply tell a
daughter in similar straits to "dump the guy" and
come home—after all, she could always find another

man.

In one of our counties I set up a child development center to care for preschool children and help them get off to a good start in life.

One Friday evening, I noticed this little fella standing outside the school waiting for someone to pick him up.

He was crying.

I went up to his teacher, who was holding him by the hand, and asked, "Why is he crying?"

"Oh, you see, he doesn't know which father is going to pick him up today," she answered. "He doesn't know what house he's going to spend the weekend in. The uncertainty makes him so unhappy that he cries."

The problem of that little boy is not that he doesn't have enough to eat, or doesn't have a house, or doesn't have clothes, but that he doesn't have family in the way God intended.

He isn't sure where he really belongs.

Another time, a young man named David came to help me as a volunteer. David's parents had been married for about 25 years. While their son was with me, they notified him that they were seeking divorce. Only a few months later, David's mother announced that she had already made plans to marry again.

This young man came to me in the quiet of evening

and poured out his heart. "What can I do?" he asked. "They have been my whole life, they have been my parents, and now as I begin my own life, they are saying they no longer care about each other. I don't know what to do! Who should I love? And who should I not? Who should I side with?"

The young man was so upset by his parent's divorce that he developed a stutter that, as far as I know, he still has today.

David came to me for answers, and I couldn't give him any because the answer was the very thing he was losing: family.

I am convinced that family is the magic cure, the wonder drug to end our poverty and our unhappiness.

The "laboratories" where we work to produce this strong medicine are here in CAP's programs.

Our Family Life Services program provides temporary shelter and much-needed counseling to adults and their children.

Our youth centers and teen centers address teen pregnancy and sexuality, substance abuse, and dropout prevention.

Our Adult Education program helps young adults gain the skills needed to get a job and manage a household, and shows them options other than too-early marriage and unwed motherhood.

It is also in our child development centers. When we opened the first of our six centers in 1974, the focus was primarily on children. Today, we focus on the entire family in our goal to break the cycle of poverty and despair.

Yes, we hold the Wonder Drug in our hands—we just need the means to administer it to those in need.

The answer to poverty is not just economic aid. It is a good, well-prepared, God-centered marriage with both father and mother—and the strong family that is the result of their love.

Dear Loving Father in Heaven, You told us to ask and we shall receive. I ask for your great gift of family. I ask that you bestow that gift of family on the people in need here in Appalachia, on the employees and volunteers of CAP, and on all those who support us from afar. Please give them all the gift that is the only cure for so many of our ills: family.

Family: A True Jewel, But It Needs Polishing

One day I visited a family living in a crowded, dilapidated shack. They had no running water. They used an outhouse.

I told them about our Home Repair program. I asked them how we could help.

The couple told me they needed a larger kitchen and a bathroom. We worked long and hard with them to add these essentials to their home. Things went well for a time and I thought we had set them on a good path.

Some months later the couple split and soon after divorced.

The house was larger and better, but empty. There was no light inside, no life.

Family was gone.

Once again, we had given much while failing to meet the greatest need: the repair of the family itself.

Not long after that, we began recruiting counselors who had the religious background and the social skills to guide such families through troubled times.

When we met with a family, our first concern was with the mother and the father. Did they really know each other? Were they aware of the other's needs? Could they go beyond themselves?

It was revealing how often they only saw their own needs and desires. "Love," we told them, "is the desire to help and care and give to someone else more than you care or want for yourself." Often we found that the husband didn't know his wife's most pressing needs and desires. What were her dreams? What would she love to have for the house? How did she imagine the future?

Before long, we'd discover a smile when we visited the home, a mother's face brightened by the gift of a new dress, if only an inexpensive one. The dress brought her joy not so much because she needed it, but because the father had thought to give it to her. Of course, there were still problems, but now they were working together on them. They were becoming a partnership. And this was wonderful.

We also discovered how little parents knew about raising children. They knew, of course, that children were to be fed and clothed and housed and schooled.

But they knew little about how to help their children grow emotionally and spiritually.

They didn't know how to discipline their children. Some of them thought a good beating was the only way. Others spoiled their children completely. Some did both.

Once I tried to purchase a piece of property for a new church. On the property was a house that was in bad shape and had been empty for a year.

I called upon the owners, and the woman told me the property and the house had belonged to her husband's parents. She told me they could certainly use the money because they were deeply in debt, but she'd have to talk to her husband. She suggested I return the next day.

When I came back, I was informed that the property was no longer for sale. The couple's ten-year-old daughter had heard her parents talking about selling and screamed and jumped up and down. She didn't want them to sell Grandma's house. As much as the family needed the money, they gave in.

That child ran the house. And they suffered for that.

I have seen children in grocery stores picking things off the shelves. When their mother says no, it makes little difference—the item is in hand.

"Don't you open that!" the mother screams.

Off comes the wrapper.

"Look what you've done, I'll have to buy it now!" the mother groans. The child laughs and runs down the next aisle to do it all over again.

It saddens me to see such inability to discipline. That child will grow up to think that he or she can do anything without repercussions.

Schools in Appalachia have some of the poorest attendance records in the nation. Often it is because the kids don't want to go to school. They say they are sick. As soon as the school bus has gone down the road to the next stop, the child is miraculously cured.

When parents visit our child development centers they are often amazed to see how the children obey and do as they are told. "How do you get them to do that?" they ask the teacher.

Out of such experiences—and such questions— we developed parenting classes to share with mothers and fathers the best information available from experts in the field.

"Discipline doesn't mean that you don't love," we explain. "It means that you love enough to bring out the best in your child."

Another element often surprisingly lacking in families is the value of work. In our society we have come to believe that everyone has a right to whatever they need. It is owed to them.

I don't share that belief. I grew up in a very poor family, during the Great Depression. My parents didn't sit back and wait for handouts. They saw to it that everyone pitched in and worked to make the burden a little lighter for us all.

Just recently, two women came to me. They were fine people, working hard to help the poor. As I loaded up the clothing, the food, and the other items from Operation Sharing that they were taking back with them for the poor, I asked about their distribution system.

"Oh, we give everything away," said one. "We would never expect the poor to give anything back."

I looked at her with sorrow.

"Do you have such a low opinion of the poor?" I asked. "Do you think of them as second class citizens who have to be treated like children? Why do you want to enslave them and act as if they had no resources or values of their own to help them stand on their feet? Why do you take away the pride they so desperately need?"

She looked back, shocked. "Why, I only wanted to help them!" she said.

"Then let them work, even as you worked to help them," I said. "Give them the opportunity to be free and to help create their own solutions."

At CAP we say to those who come to us, "Yes,

you can have the $50 or $75 you need for your electricity, or your heat, or your water, or your medicine.
But we want you to work the amount out."

More often than not, they agree. In one area we
serve, we've received hundreds of hours of work in
return for our help. Not only did these people benefit by the things we gave them, they worked to benefit still others who needed help.

A family that knows the value of work is well on
its way to happiness.

Teaching children discipline and the value of work
is not enough to make these families whole. They
need to live each day knowing they are cherished
members of the family of God.

The other day I met a gentleman who said to me,
"You know, I envy you. God listens to your prayers.
He never listens to mine. He doesn't like me."

"How do you know he doesn't like you?" I asked.

"Because that's the way I feel. If He liked me,
things would be going better."

I thought, what a strange isolated world this man
has created for himself! He doesn't know God loves
us all, especially those of us who are sinners. He
doesn't know God will leave ninety-nine of His sheep
to search for the one who is lost and needs finding.

A great, but invisible, part of the poverty here is
this great sense of isolation. The people believe no

one cares—not even God. So why try any more?

One of the things we do in some of our programs is to give the people we care for a cross with a little sign that says, "God so loved you." We ask them to put it up in their home, so that every time they see it they will know they are not alone—that in fact they are the object of the greatest love.

A part of nearly every visitation with our elderly is prayer and reading from the Bible. If for some reason the volunteer forgets to pray, the elder often says, "We didn't pray yet! We have to talk to Him before you leave, you know."

When this happens, I think to myself, we have given them more than a visit. We've given them God's love.

I have spent nearly 50 years preaching outdoors. I have gone into places where there were no churches, along railroad tracks or outside general stores, in front of post offices, wherever people congregate. I talk to them about their best friend, the Lord Jesus. Often people come up to me saying, "I haven't been in church for years, but this is the most exciting thing I've experienced for many a day. You have brought God up our creek and in our holler!"

Maybe the most significant thing I have done in all my years in Appalachia is that I keep saying, "God loves you, God cares, God forgives. And He seeks to have you at His side."

Family with God is the only full family. It is the only family that is whole.

There are so many other ways that we try to build and strengthen the family. We gave out more than 2,000 baskets of food, clothing and toys this past Christmas to families scattered all over the mountains, for example.

But I would rather say, "We changed the outlook—the focus—of a hundred families. In these hundred families, we kindled a spark and a vision of how they could build a family with God. Through this we brought love, dedication, and discipline. Those families are now transmitting this wisdom to their children and to their grandchildren."

Dear God, please use our efforts to show Your people Your love and set them free. With Your love, these families will endure long after the Christmas baskets are gone. Please help them through family, the jewel You polished and blessed.

How Big Should My Family Be?

When I was a young man, I imagined a family of a dozen sons and daughters.

When I was called to the priesthood, I thought of my family as the members of my Catholic faith—the parish to which I was assigned, the diocese of which I was a part, all the Catholics of Appalachia and finally of the world.

The horizons stretched out even further as the years rolled on. The community in which I lived, the state, and the country as a whole became part of that family as well. As time went on and I grew wiser, I realized I had a kinship with all of Christianity, no matter what its varied traditions and rituals. Volunteers, employees, and supporters of CAP's work from all denominations were my family.

Now that I am old and my final home is just around the bend in the road, I realize what a gift God has bestowed on me. I asked for a family of a dozen and

He gave me thousands.

My Catholic heritage has always meant much to me, but in my early years I didn't realize how caring this Catholic family was.

When I first came to the mountains in 1950, I needed people to build and paint and clean up. I needed strong backs and willing hearts. I thought of the boys I had taught at Newport Catholic High School. I had passed most of them—surely they owed me something, I thought! To my joy many of the boys came and lived with me for a summer and helped me in a hundred ways.

The parish of St. Bernard in Dayton, Kentucky, where I first served, remembered me as well. They prayed for me, they sent donations, and even donated a church bell for my first chapel.

Then, like a spring rain, other strong, powerful parishes in the diocese responded. Children collected food and toys, adults sent me building materials and household items. They took up collections. One parish even donated a used car.

Our first permanent volunteer came from a parish in Covington, Kentucky. (We refer to volunteers who stay for a year or more as "permanent volunteers.")

It wasn't long before members of this extended Catholic family from Ohio, Michigan, Illinois, New York, Pennsylvania, Massachusetts, Maryland, New

Jersey, California, Florida, Texas, and all the places in between began to come to work with me. They didn't know me personally, but we had a bond of faith.

Last May, I met Pope John Paul II in Rome. I told him I had spent 45 years in Kentucky's Appalachian Mountains. He squeezed my hand hard and with a strong voice said, "God bless you, keep it up."

That blessing was for all of us—all our family.

From the youngest child to the oldest woman, from seminarians and priests, from bishops and cardinals to the Pope, I have found strength and support from this wonderful Catholic family.

I've found family in other communities as well— although it seemed unlikely at first.

When I first came to Berea, a neighbor who had a negative view of Catholics started a petition to bar me and the Catholic Church from the town.

Twenty years later, in a community meeting about bringing industry to the town, the same gentleman got up and said, "I tried to get this man thrown out when he first came to Berea. Today I am very pleased that I didn't succeed. Father is the only preacher in town worth a dime."

I wish he had set the value a little higher than a dime! But while I knew he was wrong about the other ministers, I was proud to hear him welcome me into the Berea family.

I lived in Lancaster for 31 years. There I founded the Christian Appalachian Project, built a Catholic church and school, started a camp for children, and much more.

But what really sticks out in my memory of Lancaster was the small African American community. The people who lived there were poor, hard-working, and often despised members of our community.

I always stood with them and made them a part of every program I began. Some time after I left Lancaster, I returned for a meeting. Several of my black friends saw me driving through town. They called, "Hey Father! Pull over. We want to talk to you."

I pulled over and we talked. As we parted after a long conversation, one of them said, "Father, you know, Lancaster isn't the same since you left."

I was family.

There were other towns. I didn't have the opportunity to live in each and every one of them. I might be there preaching out of doors, or talking to the Rotary Club or the Chamber of Commerce. Sometimes I was there starting a new program to help the needy.

In all these towns, a bond was created. The people knew how much I cared for them, how hard I worked to get the things they needed.

I gathered up everything I could. I don't ever re-member turning down a single thing, because I knew somewhere, someone could use it.

I had to build warehouses, rent buildings, purchase trucks and hire people in order to take in all the do-nations of material things!

Today, trucks unload almost daily. Their goods are sorted, stored, and then distributed, often through Operation Sharing.

In 1995, we helped over 1,000 churches, charities, social agencies, and community groups by sharing the goods donated to us. We now distribute about $20 million in food, books, clothing, furniture, and other goods every year. I hope that by the year 2000, this program will have grown to $50 million per year.

CAP has helped start several private schools—we've donated books, desks, blackboards, other fur-niture, and even cash. Often I get notes and draw-ings from the children, telling me how much they appreciate what they have received and how they pray for me and ask God to bless me.

I have found family with these little ones, and with their parents and teachers as well.

We often receive donations of medical supplies and equipment. We immediately funnel these to public health clinics in our area. The clinics once sent me a plaque in gratitude. It made me feel like part of their family.

Food is an ever-present need in Appalachia. Thank goodness I have a family of friends who share surplus food. We sort it and make it available to other organizations. When people come to pick up the food they often ask, "How can we repay you?"

I tell them, "Treat all the people you meet as if they are your family, for surely they are."

I pray each day that more corporations in America will learn of what we are doing and send their surplus inventory and overstocked items to us to help build and sustain this family of God.

I can't end this chapter without paying special attention to the family that unites me with my brothers and sisters in almost every Christian denomination in our land.

In the beginning this was not an easy family to enter. I grew up in an area that was predominantly Catholic and in Appalachia found myself in an area that is thoroughly Protestant.

Old feelings, old misunderstandings, old prejudices are hard to lay aside, whether you are Catholic or Protestant. I have been shot at, hit by tomatoes, cursed, run off the road, and arrested, put on trial, and found guilty (the ridiculous conviction was later overturned) just because I am Catholic. I suffered much from being rejected and treated like some dangerous critter.

I am sure, too, that at times my lack of knowledge of my non-Catholic neighbors and their religious traditions was part of the problem. I had my shortcomings—as did all my Catholic confreres.

But I was determined to do more than just make friends. I wanted to be a brother to every religion in our land. I knew this meant that at times I had to be silent. I had to learn to absorb.

Scripture says that by patient endurance we shall be saved. I waited and prayed for that patient endurance. I knew I had to take the first steps. The first hand out in friendship had to be mine. I was the stranger, the alien. I had to show that I came in love and in friendship.

The first thing I did was to publicly acknowledge the debt I felt—and that the Catholic Church felt—to those Protestant missionaries who had done so much in Appalachia to praise the name of the Lord and help His people.

John Fee, who started Berea College, was a Baptist minister. The Baptist churches throughout Appalachia have constantly kept the word of God alive and well.

The Dutch Reformed Church built the first hospital and the first private school in Jackson County.

They gave God a good name. I was proud of them for that.

The Methodists had schools, churches, and thrift stores all over Appalachia. The great religious revivals of the early 1800s were due to these fine people. How could one talk about Appalachia and not give them credit?

The Presbyterian Church has always sought to put theology into practice. The impact of their learned and dedicated ministers has lasted nearly 200 years.

All the other churches, too numerous to mention by name, brought a special sense of God, morality, and personal responsibility to the people of the mountains.

My Catholic Church came much later. We had much to thank our Protestant brothers and sisters for. They toiled when we were not yet there.

After expressing gratitude for their work, I asked them how I could be of help to them. "Did they need chairs for the choir? Pews for the congregation? Shingles for the roof? Tile for the floor? Insulation for the walls?"

I had it—and they could have it free.

At first I sensed reluctance and suspicion among the churches. What was I after? What was I trying to do? Who was I trying to control? Then the barriers fell and we were partners. Whatever I had, I shared—

books, food, or any other thing under God's high heaven.

Then I began to hire ministers to help carry out the goals of CAP. Who better to bring the love of Christ to His people than these wonderful men and women who made up the ministry?

Right now CAP has several Protestant ministers assisting in many ways to build and deepen family life. I have been humbled by the ways they have welcomed me into their midst. In public meetings they tell hundreds of people how priests and Protestant ministers have become one, giving complete respect and dignity to each other.

As I look back on the vast variety of things I have been involved in, I think this building of family between the great variety of God's people in other churches may be the finest.

God, help all Christians to come together in the work of Your Son for Christian family life. We know there is still healing to be done, but like a good family we are working on it. Please give us the strength and perseverance to see this work through.

Judi Jackson

*Imagine the stress of caring for younger siblings
when you are only a child yourself!*

Yes, some families in Appalachia live in conditions as deplorable as these.

Her future is directly linked to the strength of her family.

Beth Dotson

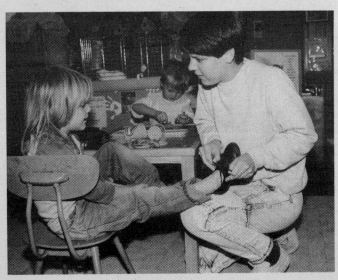

Jeff Rogers

We try to instill a love of learning at an early age.

Lorraine Corsale

Beth Dotson

Their beautiful faces mask the poverty they live with every day.

CAP Archives

Elderly visitation remains a cornerstone of CAP's outreach programs.

A fun-filled week at camp works wonders for poor Appalachian children.

Our Christmas Basket Program brightens the lives of thousands of poor Appalachian families.

Judi Jackson

*Produce and pride -- two offshoots of our
garden seed program.*

The fierce pride of the Appalachian people sometimes makes it difficult for them to accept help. That's why we always offer a hand <u>up</u> not a hand<u>out.</u>

Volunteers: The Story of Adoption

Ordinarily a mother and a father are the ones who adopt another's child as their own.

In my case, the opposite has happened. Many people from all walks of life, of every age and place, have come here to Appalachia and adopted me—and called me "Father." Adoption has created a new family for me. What a wonderful family it is!

The first folks to adopt me were from Cincinnati. Rita and Al and their children had been friends of my own family for years. When my Great Aunt Rose and my cousin Mildred came down to help me start a camp for children, Rita and Al occasionally visited us to help out at the camp.

Then tragedy struck. Al died of a heart attack. The oldest child had married but there were still four others at home. As spring approached, Rita asked me if she could come down and cook for the children at the camp. She felt getting involved would be good for her and her family. I told her to get here as soon as she could.

When summer ended, I forgot to tell her that camp was over—and she stayed on, year round, for ten years. Her children grew up as part of the volunteer group, and she became a second mother to the college students and all the others in our volunteer family.

When I was in Boston on the trip I mentioned earlier, several former volunteers arranged for me to go to speak to about 125 former Christian Appalachian Project volunteers. Some had been with me in Appalachia 30 years ago and some had been there as recently as last summer. It was a marvelous evening—with an unusual twist.

Two volunteers told me there was a surprise 40th birthday party going on for another former volunteer in Lancaster, Kentucky.

The "birthday boy" and his wife had met and fallen in love as CAP volunteers. I had celebrated their wedding. Now they have five beautiful children.

"Let's call them up!" suggested the volunteers from Boston, "and wish Steve a happy birthday!"

We called and when I wished Steve a happy birthday, he couldn't believe it. "Where are you," he asked, "in Louisa?" (Louisa, Kentucky is where I now live.)

"No," I said, "I'm in Boston with a group of former volunteers and we just thought it would be wonderful to call you and let you know we thought of you on this important day."

That's what family is about—caring for one another even when separated by years and miles.

Not long ago I got an overseas call from a priest. He was stationed in Japan, and made regular visits to Korea. He was coming back to America, and he wanted to visit me in Kentucky. Long ago, during his seminary days, he had spent three summers with me, street preaching and visiting people out in the mountains.

He said, "You know, I don't think you fully appreciate what you did for us when we were here, how we became a part of a family. That summer, I was thinking of quitting the seminary. I felt God was calling me to something else. After working with you that summer, with the cohesiveness that we felt living in that trailer, and preaching on those highways, and praying together at night, I once again heard the calling to this family. I continued my studies. And I want you to know that the things that I do in Japan, and the help that I bring to Korea, are only there because of the family you began in Kentucky."

What a wondrous thing family is! You don't have to know how it works, and you don't have to know where it goes. All you have to do is love enough to make it happen.

During my trip to Rome last spring, a priest friend and I decided to make a little eight-day trip. In Ulm, Germany, there is a professor who had helped me a great deal when he lived in Chicago and taught me at DePaul University. I called him and asked if he could help arrange our trip.

He did so with great delight.

He said, "When you leave Rome, come up through Florence and then to Venice. Right outside of Venice there's a former CAP volunteer. You can stay with him!"

We spent one night at that volunteer's home before heading off to Germany to stay with Hans. From there we visited a seminary in Bavaria where Hans had taught, and the seminarians there marveled at the stories of our Appalachian Mountains.

I also had something to marvel at. How, I thought, in the name of all that is holy, can I find roots in Venice, and Ulm, and in France?

The roots of our family of volunteers have spread throughout the world!

Its branches have also reached quite high. Back in the United States, I was invited to give the Benediction for the groundbreaking ceremony for a new business complex to be built in Somerset, Kentucky. Our

U.S. Representative was there. We had a nice visit and he went back to Washington and I back to Louisa. On Tuesday I received a letter from him asking, "Why didn't you tell me you have friends in such high places? The other day I had a visit from the Director of the FBI, Louis Freeh. He asked me if I knew where Rockcastle County, Kentucky was. I said, 'Why of course. But how do you know where Rockcastle County is? You're a New York State man.'

" 'Oh,' he said, 'when I was in high school I spent a summer with Father Beiting as a volunteer.' "

The head of the FBI had scribbled a little note to me and the Congressman had included it with his letter. Mr. Freeh wrote to thank me for that summer, because it had helped shape his own life.

In April, 1995, I went to Washington and visited with Mr. Freeh. What amazed me most was how he remembered the Sunday evenings when I gathered all the volunteers from all our counties together to spend a couple hours in prayer and song. We would talk about the work we had done that week and our plans for the future. I thought, "Beiting, you'll have to be more careful what you say to volunteers from now on. They remember everything."

Sometimes sorting out the volunteer family from the Catholic family gets a little confusing. A man who had been with us phoned me to ask if I'd be willing to preach at his church on Sunday. I assumed he was a Catholic, so I said, "Yes, I'll be glad to do that. What time are the Masses?"

He said, "Oh Father, we don't have Masses! We just have preaching and scripture and singing. I belong to the Church of God in Worcester, Ohio."

I said, "Well, I'm sorry I made that mistake—but I am still honored to come!" I went and talked to them about our work and our needs.

Just recently, they returned the visit with two tractor trailers, one loaded completely with food, and the other with furniture, toys, and household items of every kind.

Out of the confusion of my own ignorance came a gift. Sometimes you get mixed up with who is your family and who isn't. But God knows we're all brothers and sisters.

My family of volunteers doesn't always come bringing things. Sometimes it asks for things.

Just last week I got a call from Arliss Beavers, who had been a CAP employee for several years. He is a minister of the Church of God in Kentucky. He was trying to collect various items that could be used by their congregations in Ohio, West Virginia, and Tennessee. He was beginning to have some success, but he had nowhere to store the donated goods.

He wanted to know if I could find a trailer he could

use temporarily to store the items as they came in.

I thought, "Now we really are a family." It's not only the kids giving something to the parents, but the parents are asked to do something for the kids. It's truly a family in the fullest sense of the word.

I assured Arliss that I would find him a trailer, and he could have it to continue his wonderful work.

What really amazes me are the former volunteers who come to visit. Louisa, Kentucky is not exactly the center of the world. But I get visits from many, many people. They call and say, "Can we stop by?"

It's only a couple hundred miles out of the way to see me. They come, as all families come. Often they bring gifts for the poor.

Sometimes I'm just a little too far out of the way, so they write. I recently opened a letter from Bill and Kathy Brunscheen of New York. Bill started in 1987 as a temporary volunteer at Camp Shawnee. Later he accepted the challenge of a one-year commitment as a permanent CAP volunteer.

"I remember the first time I saw you," Bill wrote. "You came one evening to address the new volunteers during our orientation. Your message was clear: We were all here in Appalachia to serve God and NOT to be humanitarians. That is what set CAP apart from other groups who had come to Appalachia to 'give to the poor.' That was not your plan. You challenged us to be people and communities of prayer, and to rely on God for our strength and the love that we were called to share with the people we would be serving.

"Being a volunteer with CAP was one of the best experiences of my life. I learned so much about God, myself, and others. Like many others, I also ended up marrying another CAP volunteer.

"Kathy and I have been blessed with two beautiful children. Just as you taught us to make God the center of our CAP community, Kathy and I continue each day to invite God into the center of our family.

"Living in community as a CAP volunteer, I learned first-hand how different we are, and all created by God. The experience taught me how to respect others and to learn from them. Now that I am a parent, I see how God has brought even our own children into this world with their own individual personalities and styles. Even though we are different, with God at the center of our family we trust that we can grow to be all that we have been created to become.

"I will never forget the day you asked to come with me on my visit to James and Gladys, an elderly couple who lived in a holler in the mountains. Even though you were the founder of CAP, you sat on the floor with the rest of us and listened to those simple people talk about their needs. You prayed with them, and I watched the love on your face and the tears in your eyes and I knew what the true love of family was all about."

Bill's letter brought such joy to my heart—for he clearly shares my vision of family, and my deep desire to bring God into the center of the families of Appalachia.

I also get notes from the elderly people who have volunteered with us. They often write to apologize for not sending clothes and other items. They tell me they can't move around so well anymore. But they still want to pray for me, and they want me to know they are asking God each day to remember me in love.

What would a family be like if there were no prayer and sacrifice involved?

I enjoy being an adopted member of this volunteer family. My biological family had no choice but to stick with me. But these wonderful volunteers have adopted me—by choice—with all my shortcomings.

I guess I'm selfish enough to wish this volunteer family would grow even larger. I need so many more volunteers! Old or young, of any religious background . . . I want them all.

I suppose I do have a few restrictions for those who come here to volunteer in person. (There are no restrictions whatsoever for those who want to pray for me.) The rigors of working in the mountains demand reasonably good health. I need people with a deep sense of love for God, the desire to work in an unselfish manner to assist others, and the willingness to be part of a team—a family.

That is the kind of family I need. I guess you could say there's an old man down here in the hills who has still many more miles to travel—and who would like to be ˈdopted.

God, please send more volunteers to adopt me. I need family more than ever. I need their enthusiasm. I need their determination. I need their courage. I need their love.

Donors: The Family I Rarely See

We all have members of our families whom we rarely see. Distance has taken them away from us. We seldom see them but they are real, supporting us in many ways. We get notes or letters from them. They call us. We know they love us.

Like everyone else, I have days when I feel nobody cares, my troubles are limitless, and hope is a mirage.

When I feel this way, I find a quiet spot and think about the family I haven't seen lately.

Right now I'm remembering an old woman who sent me a note saying she was only able to send five dollars for my work. She knew it wasn't much, but it was all she had. She would have spent it on medicine, but she said, "I'll do without medicine for the rest of the month so you can care for someone in greater need."

I wouldn't suggest that others imitate this sacrifice without a doctor's advice, but I was amazed at her love. I had never seen this woman face-to-face yet she went to such lengths to help me. She, at least, cared. She hadn't forgotten about me.

I shall never forget her.

One day when worries were wearing me out, I decided to give away a couple of pictures. Someone had given me two large, beautiful pictures, one of Jesus and one of Mary, His mother. They were without frames, but another friend had given me two beautiful gold frames to fit those pictures. I attached the pictures to the frames and went to the house of a nearby family.

When Sarah answered the door, I said, "I was thinking of you and Michael and your children because I haven't seen you for some time, and I just thought perhaps you might enjoy these pictures."

In a fearful voice, Sarah told me that Michael had been sick. He had gone through tests at a number of clinics but the doctors had been unable to pinpoint the problem. They were all discouraged.

My visit cheered them up. They said it felt great to know that someone cared enough to bring two beautiful pictures to their home, for no reason other than friendship.

"I shall not forget this," Michael said.

Only a week later, I received a call from Michael.

"I wanted to let you know that I can get food for your work. The cases are broken, but the cans and boxes inside are perfectly fine. I think I can get you some every week."

We worked out the details and now this wonderful arrangement has been going on for months. Every Wednesday there is another shipment to pick up—from a friend, from a donor, from a family that I rarely ever see, who responded so generously to my simple gift.

I'm overwhelmed and filled with joy.

Not long ago, I was in the Cincinnati area. I had a couple of free hours and I remembered a friend I hadn't seen for a year or so. I decided to stop by at his business, just to let him know that I pray for him, and to remind him of how much I have appreciated his past help for CAP.

He only had a few minutes to spare because he had another appointment, but he wanted to know what he could do to help. I told him we needed building materials to finish construction of our new summer camps, a home for people with disabilities, and a number of other projects.

"We've had a good year," he said. "I don't see why we can't help out. How much do you need?"

I said, "Could I have two trailer loads?"

"I think you can. Let me work on it."

The other day he called me to tell me that one trac-tor-trailer would be down in two weeks, and the other will be down within the month.

I hadn't seen this friend in so long. A simple act of kindness, of stopping by and letting him know that he was remembered with love, created a new cycle of love and generosity.

Wonderful things happen because of family you rarely see.

Recently, I met a woman from South Carolina who was in the area. She had been a contributor for some years, but this was the first time I had an opportunity to meet her face-to-face.

She told me about a friend of her daughter—a young girl whose father was a well-to-do gentleman out West. The man ran the third largest cheese-pro-ducing business in the United States.

My friend said, "This gentleman has sent teams to Russia and to China, trying to get them to use his ideas to create jobs making cheese. What if we could get him to start in Appalachia as well? I have been so thrilled by your work, and inspired by your books. Here is a way we might be able to start jobs!"

She is now contacting her daughter, who will con-tact the businessman's daughter, and hopefully I will soon go out West to visit the gentleman and see if we can't start something new.

The prospect is so exciting. What if this should work? It would be the most significant addition I could ever make to this county! It might help the people stand on their own and look at the rest of the country with pride.

All because of a member of my family, a supporter in a faraway state, whom I had never met until recently.

Economic development is one of CAP's most important goals—and so far, one of the most elusive. We are constantly trying to draw new businesses to Appalachia. The excuses many give are, "The people aren't educated, they can't be skilled workers."

So we are committed to enrolling men and women in our adult education programs.

Dora was one of 114 students who earned a General Education Diploma (GED) last year. This 18-year-old from Berea, Kentucky earned it after joining our Infant and Toddlers: Parent Connections program. Like many girls, she'd dropped out of school to have her baby. She felt she didn't belong in school after the baby was born.

Dora's life could have continued spiraling downward, but at Infant and Toddler: Parent Connections, she received encouragement and support. She made friends with other moms. Together, they found solutions to common problems. Most important for Dora, she found acceptance and love.

With new confidence, Dora began studying for her GED. "I never thought I'd really wear one of these!" she exclaimed on graduation night, as she showed off her cap and gown.

CAP is helping many more students study for their GED this year.

We have no educated people? We have no skilled workers? America, come and see!

Right now I'm trying to acquire some land that is owned by a coal company. There are three buildings on this land. They haven't been used for seven or eight years.

I would love for this coal company to donate the property to CAP. They would get a tax credit, and we could use the space to create new businesses that will employ people from our area.

I talked to the management of the coal company. I wrote letters and phoned them, but I didn't seem to be getting anywhere.

I decided to write to the governor of our state. I had met him on several occasions and he was impressed and grateful for what CAP was doing.

I said, "Governor, will you write to this coal company and tell them what good things could happen by their generosity?"

He assured me that he would.

Then I contacted one of our representatives in Washington and asked him the same thing. And he said, "You bet I will!"

A few days later, I received a phone call from the coal company.

"My, you have powerful friends!" the manager told me. "We're going to think about this again and hopefully we'll have an answer for you in the near future."

I hope by the time this book is published they'll have made up their minds—and made the right choice.

Even people in high places, in our state capitals and in Washington, D.C., are reaching out with love to help us. They're part of the CAP family, too. Like our supporters, they're trying to help me create permanent and ongoing hope in Appalachia.

The unseen members of one's family often bring about more good than those we see and meet every day. I gave a talk in a community to the north of here, and one of the things I mentioned was how difficult it was to continue our programs to help the poor without a decent truck.

We had a couple of trucks in that area, but they were old and dilapidated. We had prayed over them, kicked their tires, and used a few words that aren't in the scriptures—and they still didn't always want to go.

Not long after that talk I received a phone call, from another man I hadn't seen for years.

"I heard you need a truck," he said, "I'll be sending one down—a 16-foot box bed truck. Used, of course. But it runs great."

Once more, someone who hadn't seen me for a long time, and yet heard of the need, came forward with love.

I recently received a letter from a Catholic sister who had been one of my teachers many, many years ago. I knew she had retired from teaching and used a wheelchair. She could do a few odd jobs around the convent, but spent most of her time in the chapel.

Her note simply said, "I have written down all your names, you and the others that I taught, and when I go to Chapel I bring out my notebook and go through it, and I see the names and pray for them. When I see yours I pray a little harder than I do for the rest, because you always seemed to me to need prayers more than the rest. But I'm impressed by what you are doing and I think that deserves more prayers as well."

I wonder how many others are out there—how many elderly folk who can't do much except pray and offer up their sacrifices and love? Good people saying to God, "Take care of him, watch after him, help him to bring about the good that you want done"?

This family is marvelous. It's beyond my power to fully understand.

I rarely see these members of my family, but I know they represent every Christian church and denomination in our land. I am so humbled when I get letters from Protestant groups, and pastors, and youth ministers, saying how grateful they are for the opportunity to assist us.

It's not only the little children or the teens, but grownups and senior citizens as well. Our family of supporters fills every age bracket. Its members are in every locality, of all different economic status. They are unable to come and work on our projects. But they help. Prayers, donations, supplies of all kinds—they all come because of this extended family. What would I ever do without them? They are my life blood—my hope—my family.

*Thank you, Lord, for this family who must live
so much by faith. They don't see us, yet they care.
Please let them know how dear to me they are,
and how close they are to me . . . as family.*

Grandfather: My New Role In This Family

God blessed me with a good memory. Going back three score and ten years and more, I can recall so many of the family members—the blood relatives, the volunteers, the supporters, and of course the people of Appalachia—that have touched and influenced my life.

There is another family that has greatly influenced my life, however, and my story of family would be incomplete without them. They are the men and women of generations before me who now rest among the blessed. Some folks call them heroes. To me they are more than that.

They are family.

I feel related to some of them because I've walked the paths they made. I occupy the same space they once filled. To my own state of Kentucky came my favorite hero of all: Daniel Boone. Not the coonskin-capped star of television, but the real and gentle man who was the father of ten. This adventurous pioneer led the way for a new nation to go west. He was a man of courage and determination. A man who was a friend of God.

Abraham Lincoln, a native of Kentucky, is another member of the family I so much admire. His concern for the poor, the oppressed, and the forgotten renews my dedication each day. I read his pronouncements and speeches, and I know I am still in a nation which is under God—where liberty and justice can be had for all.

In more recent years, other giants have occupied heroic places in Kentucky's history: women like Alice Lloyd and Jane Buchanan, who traveled to Pippa Passes in Knott County, Kentucky to make education a reality in our mountains; Mary Breckinridge of the Frontier Nursing Service, who saved the lives of so many children; and Harry Caudill, whose writings about Appalachia stirred a nation.

Politicians like John Sherman Cooper; Bert Combs; Happy Chandler; and Alben Barkley, the "happy veep" (Vice President) of the United States during Truman's term, have played a role in my family. I met them all during the course of my journey and theirs, and they brought me a sense of vitality and excitement that has been with me all the days since then.

Beyond Kentucky, men like Washington and Jefferson have been more than pages in history for me. I admire their courage, their wisdom and their perseverance. They influence me as much as any member of my family ever has.

I am also deeply in debt for the religious inspiration I have gained from so many people who lived a very long time ago.

When I read the story of Patrick and his gift of faith to Ireland, I am moved to keep my journey going no matter what the cost.

Bernard of Clairvaux, that incredibly eloquent and dedicated monk, stirred a tired France and brought about a religious revival that ended the Dark Ages.

Francis, that wonderful man of Assisi, gave the world—and me—a vision of how we must treat the created world.

Thomas More of Henry the VIII's England reminded me that while we must be the king's loyal servants, we must be God's first. He showed how the world of politics and faith could merge in a beautiful way.

Ignatius of Loyola, that wonderful soldier of Spain, showed me there was a better army or a society to belong to. The Jesuits who follow him still change the world.

One of them, Francis Xavier, crossed half a world

to bring the Good News of Christ to other lands. He died alone off the coast of China, but his image is always in my mind. Every time when I think there is no way to take another step, I recall him, and I go on.

Teresa of Avila, that wonderful Carmelite nun of Spain, left such a legacy of prayer and union with God that I will always be enriched by her and her life.

Turning to America, I am forever moved by the courage and dedication of missionaries such as John de Brebeuf and Isaac Jogues, who came from France to bring Christ to a new world. They ennobled both Canada and our own country with their dedication and love for the native people.

A continent away, the Franciscan, Junipero Serra, traveled the California coast and established one mission after another, despite his poor health.

These are people ingrained into my life. They are my history and my people. They may have lived more than 1500 years ago, or they may have died in my own lifetime, but they have been family to me.

Without their presence and example, I would never have dared to attempt the things I have done. They are my communion of saints, my family of heroes. They have helped to make me what I have become. I pray future generations will discover similar people in their ancestry to inspire them.

This family of God is far larger than I ever dared to think or imagine.

All these folks from days gone by—my spiritual grandparents—remind me that I shall soon join them. They remind me that my role in this earthly family is changing. I am no longer the child who was guided, no longer the young man with a dream, no longer the father who brought a family together on this earth and created many things.

I guess now you could call me a grandfather.

I no longer can be with every group, hold every child, console every hurting person, sing at every camp fire, or lead every charge.

There are younger and stronger members of the family. The daily toil—the teaching, the feeding, and the consoling—is now theirs.

Does this make me sad? Not really. Of course, I wish I could physically do as much as I could 50 years ago, but God has given me the wisdom to see another role to play. As a good grandfather, I can tell stories of what things were like in the "good ol' days."

I know the good old days shall never return, but the faith and zeal that drove us then are still available if we want them. I hear many of the local people, the workers, and the supporters tell me how they like to listen to the stories or read the books I have written.

They tell me how the history of days past has opened a more exciting future for them.

I tell all who will listen about my failures and short-comings—and how I didn't let them slow me down. In fact, the failures were often the price that I paid for success. I believe my stories give my listeners a broader vision of their own family, and of their own journey upon the walks of this life.

I also speak to them of dreams that are still to be—the hills still to be climbed.

"You mean you are still planning, designing?" they ask. The answer is yes. Oh, of course, I sit down at times to rest, to simply recall. But God hasn't brought me up this far on the mountain to rest. It is to see the Promised Land—and encourage everyone to cross over.

In a literal sense, the workers and volunteers of CAPRICE have already gone over the mountain.

For many years, CAPRICE (Christian Appalachian Project Resources for Independence and Community Employment) served adults with disabilities in Pulaski County, Kentucky.

At a recent retreat, workers took a hard look at the program and realized a new approach was needed for a new era. Increased tourism and industry in Pulaski County had brought new opportunities for employment and support for people with disabilities.

Given that CAP's mission is to serve where the need is greatest, the path was clear: to carry CAPRICE 40 miles over the mountains from Somerset to London, Kentucky—an area where over 23 percent of the population endures disability.

Moving was an enormous undertaking, but CAPRICE did more than just move last year. We also completely redesigned the program's philosophy to better match the needs of Laurel, Clay, Knox, Whitley, and McCreary counties.

People from other CAP programs met with the CAPRICE staff and provided training in such topics as Family-Focused Services, Behavior Intervention, Communication, and the Do's and Don'ts of Home Visiting.

Information about CAPRICE was given to local families by CAP's Rainbow Respite Care Center.

One of CAPRICE's first referrals was a 34-year-old man living with his mother. Jimmy had never worked before, and the caseworker sensed that his mother felt the future was grim for her son.

But with the guidance of a CAP "job coach," Jimmy now works at a local discount store. For him and his mother, CAPRICE accomplished its program goal: for the individual to be seen as a contributing member of the family.

For this man and his mother, CAPRICE has been

the answer to a prayer.

As the years have gone on, prayer has become more a part of my life. Once I looked upon it as an obligation. Now I see it as a privilege. I have found so much comfort in it. When my strength ran low, I always knew there was a greater source. I could call on God, and from there the strength would come.

I have never worried. This isn't to say I've always known the way. Most often I haven't. But I have always known that He did—and that He would see me through.

My family in Appalachia knows I have two, and often three, church services each day. They know that my day begins and ends with my prayer book. They see the rosary that hangs from the car mirror, and know that I use it. They tell me that they pray more—and enjoy it more—because of my example.

I'm beginning to see that being a grandfather has many advantages.

Also, I don't want to retire. I want to wear out. I think my conviction about that brings a sense of perseverance to the people who work with my family!

The other day some of them came to me and said, "Father, we wish you would quit. Get a little place of your own and take it easy! Enjoy the sunsets, smell the roses, feel the gentle breeze!"

I thanked them for their concern. "Oh, heck it isn't

for you!" they replied. "*We* want to take it a little
easier. We want a slower pace. But how can we get it
while you are so much involved?"

I smiled. Grandfathers are supposed to make you
feel a little uncomfortable at times!

*Thank you, Lord, for giving me such a fine fam-
ily in this present world. Thank you for giving
me the real and spiritual family of my past, to
strengthen and inspire me.*

*Thank you for giving me the years to be a
grandfather and, hopefully, the wisdom to use
them well.*

Reaching Out for Family

I never know who reads my books. We send them to our friends and supporters. Some people request extras for friends and neighbors. Other people pick them up at yard sales and flea markets, or in doctors' offices or churches.

Although I don't know exactly to whom I am writing, I hope that everyone who reads this book will be family with me, as my journey draws ever closer to its destination.

Last night I shared a turkey dinner with six old friends. As we sat around the table, I spoke of the years I've spent in Appalachia, from CAP's beginnings to the present.

Our beginning was so humble—the promise of a piece of land, and the dream of building a camp for children. And we did it.

We sometimes faced opposition. When I tried to buy an old schoolhouse to use for our Christmas wreath operation, for example, some of the local people resisted. But I persevered. Two weeks later, they opened my sealed bid—and to their great dismay, it was the highest! The result was a Christmas wreath business that gives seasonal work to many local people.

Now, as then, we need to hang on and fight for what we believe.

In my effort to make more people aware of what we're doing, we're also making a video. Recently I went with the film crew to Jackson County in eastern Kentucky, where they filmed the greenhouses, the dairy farm, the saw mill, the woodworking factory—all businesses we started there.

When we opened that Christmas wreath operation 25 years ago, there were precious few commercial jobs in Jackson County. Now, because we led the way and others followed, there are more than 1,300.

I told my friends of the street preaching I've been doing for 50 years. As I stand on the side roads, or in front of court houses or filling stations, people gather, listen, and experience God. Often they come away thirsting to do something more noble, more meaningful with their lives.

I told my friends how the ecumenical nature of our movement has grown, and how wonderful it is to see people of different faiths doing God's work side by side.

I spoke of all we're doing with families, and how we are trying to get to the core of their problems from many angles.

For example, our Garden Seed program gives families and elderly people seeds, seed potatoes, freezer bags, and fertilizer. With these simple tools, families grow miraculous gardens that give them great pride as well as good food.

Until recently, however, it was hard for people with arthritis or disabilities to raise a garden. But Harv, a new participant in our Garden Seed program, has found an answer. He is involved with a company that makes "wall gardens:" large cubes with holes in their sides. Harv told us how he took some home, filled them with synthetic soil and fertilizer, and added seeds for green peppers, beans, and tomatoes. The produce emerged from the tops and sides of the cubes. No bending or weeding was required—and Harv ended up with more vegetables than he could use!

We hope to see more "wall gardens" blooming in Appalachia this year. It is just one more example of how a family opens itself up to every member.

The Outreach program is often the first encounter people have with CAP. As their trust in us grows, they may turn to CAP for help with more personal problems—such as the difficulties of raising a child with a disability.

Kentucky has more than its share of birth defects—and few services available in rural areas to help the families of these children.

Last year, our Parents-Are-Teachers program provided in-home intervention and education to 221 families. Melissa's was one of them.

At age two, Melissa spoke only a dozen intelligible words. The average child speaks about 200 by that age. Our Parents-Are-Teachers worker, Leigh, recommended speech therapy for Melissa.

A speech pathologist showed Melissa's parents games, songs, and activities to use with Melissa to encourage her to speak. Melissa and her mother also participated in play groups, giving the toddler the opportunity to be with other children her age.

In just three months, Melissa added nearly 100 words to her vocabulary.

At the end of a recent home visit, Leigh heard her loudly singing what many parents have come to know as "The Barney Song."

When I learned this, I had to chuckle—for the words to the song are, "I love you, you love me, we're a happy family . . ."

Melissa shares my vision of God's family, too.

But as I sat at the table last night, talking with my friends about how CAP has grown over the years, I knew there were still too many people who don't know that we are all family.

When I was done with my recollections, one of my friends spoke up. "What's going to happen when death takes you, and your voice is no longer heard? It will all pass away. It will be nothing. It will be dust again."

This was a terrible thought. "No!" I shouted. "It will not pass away! My family will still be there— they won't forget! They'll remember the poor. They will keep the torch burning, and they'll pass it to the next generation."

Isn't that what family is all about? The father and mother work hard for a better life for the children, so that the children may better care for others in turn, generation after generation. This, I hope and pray, is how it will be with my CAP family. It will endure.

Our nation is facing one of the greatest crises it has faced since the Civil War—the crisis of the family. How can we preserve family life? How can we end violence? How can we end the problems of alcohol and other drugs?

Appalachia is going to suffer the most from these problems. CAP's resources are going to be severely tested, and our resolve questioned.

A host of charities out there are calling for help and assistance. But we Americans are not giving the percentage of income to benefit the poor that our

parents and our grandparents did. They were people
of charity. They could share. They could do without.

We do not give as they gave—and the reason isn't
always financial. It is because we aren't motivated.
We aren't inspired.

Experts say that in the next ten years, there will be
the greatest transfer of wealth from one generation
to the next that this nation has ever seen. People will
be leaving their hard-earned treasure to their families and friends.

I pray daily that much of this treasure will be left
to charitable families, such as the one I have created
here in Appalachia. If people remember CAP in their
wills, strength and stability will follow. If they remember we are all family, it will help make my vision of family a reality.

Evelyn, an unmarried teacher from New York, is
an example of the difference one person can make.
Each year before Christmas she drove down with a
load of toys, and stayed to help assemble and distribute our Christmas baskets.

One day, a letter came from a lawyer. He said
Evelyn had died—and she had left a considerable
amount of money to the family that was keeping faith
and hope alive in Appalachia. We had only shared a
few weeks together in work and prayer, but she
couldn't forget us.

Because of this wonderful woman, I was able to build the volunteer quarters I had been dreaming about. Volunteers from all over the country stay there while working on home repairs for the poor, caring for elderly people, and teaching children.

People also enrich us with material gifts.

An elderly woman here was diagnosed with Alzheimer's Disease. Her son, Jared, came to take her back to live with him in Alabama. They didn't need her car so they offered to leave it with us.

I wish that elderly woman in Alabama could see the wonderful things her generosity is doing—what beautiful trips her car is making.

It brings help and hope to children, to young parents, and to elderly persons like herself.

That's because we assigned her car to our Community Health Advocates Program (CHAP) which promotes physical, mental, emotional and environmental well-being among the people here.

CHAP's women's groups meet weekly to enjoy companionship and make crafts while learning about the issues that concern them and their families. They learn about good nutrition, personal health, and how to build self-esteem in their children.

CHAP also presents programs at schools, and talks to senior citizens about health topics such as blood pressure, safety, and Alzheimer's disease.

That donated car is racking up the miles for CHAP, transporting workers here and there. I pray the dear lady who thought of us is faring as well as her gift.

The gift of the car has done so much for us. The same could be said of a used truck, or a fork-lift, or furniture, or any of the material things we need to start businesses and help the poor.

Another gift we appreciate is prayer.

Often, when I've been fighting what seems a lost cause, a sudden reversal takes place and I wonder what changed the tide.

Some time later, I'll get a note from one of our supporters. "I was very sick last month," someone will write, "and I offered it up to God and said, 'Dear God, bless Father Beiting in his work and use this to help him succeed.'"

I know right then where my unexpected victory came from. It was the prayer of this good friend— this wonderful member of our family.

My own mother, in the closing weeks of her life, was in the hospital suffering from bone cancer. The pain was excruciating. She tried to bear with it the best she could. The nurses said, "Mrs. Beiting, why don't you just scream, why don't you slam something on the floor?"

She answered, "No, that would do no good. I shall offer it up as best I can to God, and ask Him to bless my son and the poor he cares for in those mountains."

We always need family to pray and offer suffering for us, that we may succeed.

We also need more family to be here on the local scene. We always need more volunteers. Right now we need people to help with home repair. We need people in our warehouses. Two wonderful men in their late 50s and 60s, Vincent and Willey, are there now. They work hard, driving, loading, unloading, and sorting goods. How I would love to get someone to help them!

We need more volunteers to visit the homes of the poor, to learn how we can help. We need volunteers to work with families, to teach parenting, and budgeting, and so many other things.

We desperately need people to help us create jobs. How do we make a business plan? Where do we learn marketing skills? What do we need to do to get things rolling?

There are all kinds of work to be done with the young. Our teen centers, in particular, cry out for volunteers with the wisdom and love to guide young people through troubled times.

Without question, my family needs to grow.

Nearly two thousand years ago, St. Peter wrote to some early Christians who were suffering persecution. They didn't think they could withstand the

power of Rome, but he reminded them who they
were.

He wrote, "You are . . . a royal priesthood, a holy
nation . . . a people set apart. Once you were no
people but now you are God's people."

Like those early Christians, our supporters, employees, and volunteers have more strength, more
resources, more talents than they know. They, too,
are set apart.

They are the people—the family—of God.

*Dear Lord, may this book inspire more people
to join your precious family, here in the mountains of Appalachia.*

That My Family May Live Forever

One of the most instinctive drives in human beings is the hope to live forever. We want to be immortal. The ancient Egyptians expressed this by building the great pyramids. In many other cultures we see this same drive to live beyond our allotted time.

We who have been blessed with the Christian tradition know we shall live forever. Death is but the passage into eternal life. If we die in God's love and favor, we know we shall spend eternity with Him. We shall know happiness beyond our power to describe.

Yet there is still that instinct to continue our presence on the earth. When my brother Ray, just twenty months younger than I, was dying, I asked him what was the greatest sacrifice that he was having to make.

"Not to see my grandchildren be born and raised," he answered. Ray wanted to be there for them—to tell them stories of days gone by, and to give them dreams for the future.

In the early days of my priesthood, I knew a woman who prayed with all her heart to have a child. It was Julia's greatest desire. Finally, after more than a dozen years, Julia conceived.

But her labor was extraordinarily difficult. Her child was born, but Julia herself had not long to live. I hurried to her hospital room.

To this day, I can hear her say how much she wanted to live to take care of that child.

"I want to hold him in my arms," she whispered. "I want to nurse him and give him strength. I want to guide him towards God."

I once witnessed an auto accident. I ran to help and saw a man lying on the side of the road. He was dying, but his sole concern was for his family.

"You're the only one seriously injured," I told him. "The rest are shaken up, but they're doing fine."

"Are you a priest?"

"Yes."

"Can I tell you that I am sorry for my sins?"

"You may."

As he made his contrition to God, he stopped and looked at me. "Who is going to take care of my family? I've just started to provide for them! I need more time, I don't want to leave yet . . . I don't want to leave yet."

That poor man died there by the side of the road, his wish to live denied.

Years later, I understand his words . . . and Julia's words . . . and Ray's words . . . better than ever before.

I don't want to leave before the battle is over, or the contest won. I don't want that day to come when I will no longer cross a swinging bridge, or visit a run-down cabin, or hold a child on my lap.

I want to continue to talk with families, and plan with them for the future. I want to see that there is food and clothing for this great family, and a chance for the children to attend schools that will give them a sense of excellence.

I want to build more churches in these hollows and hills, where people so need the presence of God.

I want to keep on consoling the sorrowing. I want to continue to come as peacemaker into troubled homes.

I want to see beauty replace the trash and filth that litters our roads and creeks.

I want to hear the magic of music and joyful song.

I want to see the rainbow stretch from one hillside to another.

While my common sense tells me that I, too, shall pass, and that there is no way I can be here forever, there is still this instinctive, persistent drive to provide for my family.

Perhaps there is a way that my life can last forever.

I know that a spirit remains after death. I feel my
grandfather's common sense hovering about me at
times. My father's energy is with me always. My
mother's love and dedication inspire me every day.

Yet it will take more than my spirit to continue my
work in Appalachia, and make it grow.

One day my bishop, J. Kendrick Williams, Bishop
of the Diocese of Lexington, Kentucky said, "Are
you willing to work hard enough to find a way to
contribute to the material needs of the mountain
people from now until the end of time?"

"What do you mean?" I asked—not sure that I
wanted to hear the answer.

"You could set up an endowment fund. The interest from it would enrich the people of Appalachia.
The principal would never be spent. It would continue to work forever."

Well, that certainly is one way to be immortal!

Two weeks later, the Board of The Christian Appalachian Project made a similar request.

"We know your time is running out," said one board
member. "You're now in your seventies, and we're
worried. We have to figure out a way you can last
forever."

Before I knew it, the board and the bishop were giving me my marching orders: to start an endowment fund. In the next three years, I must raise five million dollars for the church and charity needs of the area, and ten million dollars for CAP for the creation of jobs—the economic salvation that Appalachia so desperately needs.

That night when I finished my prayers, I laid aside the book and lifted my eyes to the heavens. "What are you up to?" I asked Him. "I can't raise fifteen million dollars by the time I'm seventy-five! Lord, surely you wouldn't play such a joke on me. You know me best. You know I don't have the brains or the energy to do all that!"

After much babbling and complaining, I ran out of questions. I sat in silence. Then the voice came.

"Do you remember the day you thought you wanted a dozen kids?" He asked. "Remember how I changed that and enlarged your family so you can't number them all? They are everywhere, and of all kinds. I made it work then, didn't I? Do you think I have lost my wisdom or power? You may be getting old and feeble, but I'm not!"

Once again—as always—the answer to my problem is family. The Lord gave me this large family so that the financial treasure I need may be found.

"There are many in your family who would like

you to live forever," He continued. "Their concern to keep on helping the rest of the family is as much a part of their lives as yours.

"Talk to them about the endowment, and how by contributing to it they can keep the support going year after year. A gift of ten thousand dollars in ten years will give ten thousand to support the work at hand. And yet, the original will not be touched. It will still be there, working away, providing more and more each year. In twenty-five years, the ten thousand dollars will have brought about twenty-five thousand dollars for the benefit of all the people. And the original will still be there, hard at work."

Hard at work.

Many faces came to mind at that phrase. The first was Kevin's. He approached me long ago, begging for a job. He asked me to come out to his car to see his wife and five children.

When I got to the car, he looked at me, then at them, then down at the ground.

Looking up again, Kevin said, "Do you think I want these kids to grow up and see me only as a beggar? As someone who goes around with his hand out, pleading for food?" He nodded at his wife. "Look at that woman, there! I promised to take care of her the day we were married. Now what do I do, but send her out on the first of the month to get food stamps!"

I saw the agony etched on Kevin's face. He so wanted to have a job. He so wanted to be free—to be free to be hard at work.

I thought of Mitchell. Like Kevin, he had been without means, and ashamed. I decided to give him a chance, and gave him a job in one of our woodworking establishments.

A week later I was visiting there. Mitchell brought me over to his workbench. He showed me a little bookend he had made, a chopping block, and a bookstand.

"Look at these," he said. "I think they are really beautiful!"

I looked at them, and I thought they were beautiful, too.

"I didn't realize I had such skills, that I could do such things," Mitchell admitted. "You know, Father, I have grown so much in this job. I have seen myself in a different light. I would work here for nothing. I have gained so much already."

I thought of William. His mother called me last summer. William wanted to go to school in the fall in a distant city.

"Could you find him some kind of work so he can pay his travel expenses?" she asked.

I've known this family for some time. When I first met the parents, they were tragically poor. I gave them jobs and they responded well. Now William, the oldest of their three children, was ready to enter electronics school.

He had a chance to break out of poverty—the first of his family to do so.

I couldn't tell his mother that we didn't have the money. I simply said, "Yes, I'll do it. I'll get him a job and the money to pay him each week."

William is now away at school. Hopefully, prayerfully, his story will have a beautiful ending.

There is such a great need for jobs. Jobs that will set our people free. Jobs that will fill them with pride and respect. Jobs will help build the foundation to restore the strength of Appalachia's families and end the cycle of poverty.

As we create jobs, we must also proclaim the Good News of Christ. We need to build churches where people can come together and enjoy a family reunion with God. There is too much sadness here, too much cynicism. We must bring in workers to spread that Good News—and we must bring in funds to feed and house these volunteers.

> *Dear Lord, I have to be around to meet these needs. I don't see how I can succeed and have my love last forever. But You can do more things than are dreamed of.*

I know only this: I shall try. I shall do what I can to see that my journey continues—through my family. I shall do what I can to see that my family shall live forever.

As Jesus said, "Where two or three are gathered in my name, there am I in the midst of them."
With Him we can do all things.

Epilogue

Another book comes to an end. I have shared my sense of family—a family everywhere and of all kinds.

I am what I am, on the positive side, because of a good family that raised me from birth.

I was formed by members of my family who lived centuries before me. The knowledge of what they did has inspired me all my life.

I now realize that I indeed have a family even though a wife and a dozen children have not been my personal joy. But the family of the Appalachian people has been God's gift—with sons and daughters more numerous than I could have ever brought about myself.

I have also come to see that my greatest gift to Appalachia is not the material things I've brought, but the families I helped to support in love and purpose. Yet I am wise enough to see this would never have been possible without the family of volunteers, employees, and supporters who have graced and enriched my life on every side.

I hope and pray that this work will continue even when death calls me away. I want to continue to bring family to the people, to help them gain a new foothold on life, even after my death. I want to enable them to take steps that will make them truly free.

I pray that those who have read this book will join me. Together, we can make our love last forever.

As I bring this book to a close, I wonder about the future. Like most people, I fear the unknown. I face the future with a sense of my unworthiness and frailty. But I find comfort knowing that I do not walk alone.

I have my family, scattered throughout this great land. I have the Son of God, who calls us by name to follow Him. We shall overcome because of Him. My Christian faith is the most dear and precious possession of my life. It permeates my whole being. I know I should not fear, for Christ is there. All I have to do is make sure I follow in His footsteps.

I would like to conclude with St. Augustine. I think he has said so very well what I feel in my heart: my search for God, my looking for Him, my unworthiness.

"O eternal truth, true love and beloved eternity. You are my God. To You do I sigh day and night. When I first came to know You, You drew me to

Yourself, so that I might see that there were things
for me to see. But that I myself was not ready to see
them. Meanwhile You overcame the weakness of my
vision, sending forth most strongly the beams of Your
light. And I trembled at once with love and dread.

"Late have I loved You, o beauty ever-ancient, ever
new. Late have I loved You. You were within me but
I was outside, and it was there that I searched for
You. In my unloveliness, I plunged into the lovely
things You created. You were with me but I was not
with You. Created things kept me from You, yet if
they had not been in You, they would not have been
at all. You called, You shouted and You broke through
my deafness. You flashed, You shone, and You dis-
pelled my blindness. You breathed Your fragrance
on me. I drew in breath and now I pant for You. I
have tasted You and now I hunger and thirst for more.
You touch me and I burn for Your peace."

I know now that God's peace on earth comes
through family—His family.

Yes, Lord, You must have smiled that day when I
asked for a dozen children. "Why don't you ask for
more?" You must have thought. "I can give you great
measure piled up and rolling over—if only you will
ask."

Lord, how could I have doubted You. Thank
You for such a wonderful family! Amen!

THE MOUNTAIN SPIRIT

Our bimonthly magazine, *The Mountain Spirit*, will keep you up-to-date on the work of the Christian Appalachian Project as we continue to help the people of this poverty-stricken area help themselves. In the magazine, you will also find moving, inspiring stories about the people we serve. If you would like to subscribe to this publication please complete the order form below.

THE MOUNTAIN SPIRIT Subscription Order Form

Please send me CAP's magazine *The Mountain Spirit*.

Name _____

Address _____

City _____ State _____ Zip _____

Please return this Order Form to:
Christian Appalachian Project, 322 Crab Orchard Road, Lancaster, KY 40446-0001.

If You'd Like to Know More About the Christian Appalachian Project . . .

For more information about CAP, or for additional copies of *A Family of My Own*, please write or phone us at our headquarters:
Christian Appalachian Project
322 Crab Orchard Road
Lancaster, KY 40446-0001
(606) 792-3051

Thank you for your interest and support!